JUMPING INTO JAVASCRIPT

JUMPING INTO JAVASCRIPT

© John Facey

So, are you ready to jump into the world of JavaScript? Let's get started!

PROLOGUE

JavaScript is one of the most popular programming languages in the world and is used to create interactive and dynamic web applications. It is a versatile language that can be used for a wide range of tasks, from simple scripts to complex web applications. In this book, you'll learn the fundamental concepts of JavaScript, including its syntax, data types, functions, and event handling.

As you progress through the book, you'll also learn more advanced topics such as asynchronous JavaScript, JavaScript frameworks and libraries, and modules and import/export. Along the way, you'll also learn best practices for writing maintainable and readable code.

The book is filled with examples and exercises that will help you understand and apply the concepts covered in the book. By the end of this book, you will have a solid understanding of JavaScript and the skills necessary to build your own web applications.

CHAPTER 1

INTRODUCTION TO JAVASCRIPT

Explanation of what JavaScript is and its role in web development

JavaScript is a programming language that is widely used for creating interactive and dynamic web pages. It is a client-side language, which means that it runs on the user's web browser rather than on a server. This allows for a more seamless user experience and faster response times.

JavaScript is often used in conjunction with HTML and CSS to create the front-end of a website. HTML provides the structure of the web page, CSS provides the styling, and JavaScript provides the interactivity and dynamic behavior. For example, JavaScript can be used to create form validation, animations, and interactive elements like sliders and modals.

Compared to other programming languages, JavaScript is relatively easy to learn and use. It is a versatile language that can be used for both front-end and back-end development, and it has a large and active community. It's also one of the most used languages in the world. Some of the other languages that are used for web development are: Python, Ruby, C# and Java.

To get started with JavaScript development, you will need to set up a development environment. This typically involves installing a code editor or integrated development environment (IDE) and a web browser. Some popular code editors include Sublime Text, Visual Studio Code, and Atom. Once you have your development environment set up, you can start writing JavaScript code and testing it in your web browser.

You can also use some tools that makes your development easier, for example: npm (node package manager) for package management, webpack for bundling and transpiling your code, and babel for transpiling your code to be compatible with older browsers.

In conclusion, JavaScript is a powerful and versatile programming language that is essential for creating interactive and dynamic web pages. With the right tools and a bit of practice, anyone can learn to use JavaScript for web development.

CHAPTER 2

BASIC SYNTAX AND DATA TYPES

Variables and data types (strings, numbers, booleans, etc.)

One of the first things to learn when working with JavaScript is variables. Variables are used to store data and can be declared using the var, let, or const keywords. For example:

```javascript
var x = 5;
let y = "Hello";
const z = true;
```

JavaScript has several built-in data types, including:

- Numbers (e.g. 1, 3.14, -6)

- Strings (e.g. "Hello", "Goodbye")

- Booleans (true or false)

Arrays (e.g. [1, 2, 3])

Objects (e.g. {name: "John", age: 30})

JavaScript also has several operators that can be used to perform operations on variables, such as assignment (=), arithmetic (+, -, *, /), and comparison (>, <, ==, !=). For example:

```javascript
if (x > y) {
  console.log("x is greater than y");
} else if (x < y) {
  console.log("x is less than y");
} else {
  console.log("x is equal to y");
}
```

CHAPTER 3

BROWSER AND DOCUMENT OBJECT MODEL

Objects in the browser

In order to understand how JavaScript works in web development, it is important to understand the role of the browser and the Document Object Model (DOM). The browser is the software program that displays web pages on your computer or mobile device. The DOM is a programming interface for HTML and XML documents. It represents the structure of a document as a tree of objects, which can be manipulated using JavaScript.

When a web page is loaded, the browser creates a tree-like structure of objects known as the DOM. This structure represents the elements on the page, such as headings, paragraphs, and images. The DOM provides a way for JavaScript to access and manipulate these elements.

You can access the DOM using the built-in **document** object, which represents the current web page. The **document** object has properties and methods that can be used to access elements on the page, such as `document.getElementById()`, `document.querySelector()`, and `document.getElementsByTagName()`. These methods allow you to access elements by their ID, class name, or tag name.

You can also use the DOM to add, remove, or modify elements on the page. For example, you can use the `innerHTML` property to change the content of an element, the `appendChild()` method to add a new element to the page, and the `removeChild()` method to remove an element from the page.

In addition to the DOM, the browser also provides access to other web technologies such as cookies, local storage and the web storage API, the history API and the web workers API.

It is important to note that the DOM is not part of the JavaScript language but rather a feature of the web browser. It is implemented differently in different browsers, and it is important to test your JavaScript code on different browsers to ensure that it works correctly.

Exercises:

> Research and create a simple webpage using javascript to change the content of a heading
>
> Research and create a simple webpage using javascript to add a new element to the page

- Research and create a simple webpage using javascript to remove an element from the page

- Research and create a simple webpage using javascript to access and manipulate the web storage API

This chapter provides an overview of the Browser and the Document Object Model (DOM) and how they are used in web development. It explains the built-in **document** object, how to access and manipulate elements on the page and the different web technologies that the browser provides access to. The chapter also includes some exercises for readers to research and practice manipulating the DOM and other web technologies using javascript.

CHAPTER 4
FUNCTIONS

Building blocks of logic

Functions are a fundamental building block of JavaScript and are used to organize and structure code. They allow you to encapsulate a set of instructions and reuse them throughout your code. In this chapter, you will learn about the basics of functions in JavaScript, including how to create and invoke them.

Creating a Function

In JavaScript, you can create a function using the function keyword followed by the function name, a set of parentheses, and a set of curly braces. The parentheses are used to pass in any parameters that the function will use, and the curly braces contain the code that will be executed when the function is invoked. Here is an example of a simple function that takes no parameters and returns the string "Hello, World!":

```javascript
function sayHello() {
  return "Hello, World!";
}
```

Invoking a Function

Once you have created a function, you can invoke it by using the function name followed by a set of parentheses. For example, to invoke the sayHello function, you would write:

```
console.log(sayHello());
```

This will output "Hello, World!" to the console.

Passing Parameters

Functions can also accept parameters, which are values that are passed in when the function is invoked. These values can be used within the function to determine its behavior. Here is an example of a function that takes a name as a parameter and returns a personalized greeting:

```
function greet(name) {
  return "Hello, " + name + "!";
}
console.log(greet("John"));
```

This will output "Hello, John!" to the console.

Returning Values

Functions can also return a value to the code that invoked them. In JavaScript, the return statement is used to specify the value that the function should return. For example, in the sayHello and greet functions above, the return statement is used to specify the string that the function should return.

Function Scope

Functions in JavaScript also have their own scope, which means that variables and functions defined within a function are not accessible outside of it. This allows you to create variables and functions with the same name in different functions without any naming conflicts.

Functions are a powerful tool for organizing and structuring your code. They allow you to encapsulate a set of instructions and reuse them throughout your code, making it more readable and maintainable. In the next chapter, you will learn about JavaScript's built-in objects and how they can be used to make your code even more powerful and efficient.

Exercises:

> Create a function that takes two numbers as parameters and returns the sum of those numbers.

2. Create a function that takes a sentence as a parameter and returns the number of words in the sentence.

3. Create a function that takes an array of numbers and returns the largest number in the array.

The above chapter gives a quick overview of Functions in javascript, how to create and invoke them, passing and returning parameters, function scope and some examples and exercises for the readers to practice and understand the concepts better.

CHAPTER 5
EVENT HANDLING

Handling Event Actions

Event handling is an important aspect of JavaScript development, as it allows you to create interactive and responsive web pages. Events are actions that occur in the browser, such as a user clicking a button or hovering over an element.

JavaScript provides several ways to handle events, including:

> Inline event handlers: These are added directly to HTML elements using attributes, such as onclick or onmouseover. For example:

```
<button onclick="alert('Hello World!')">Click Me</button>
```

DOM event listeners: These are added using the addEventListener() method, which allows you to attach multiple handlers to a single event. For example:

```
var button = document.getElementById("myButton");
button.addEventListener("click", function() {
  alert("Hello World!");
});
```

jQuery event handlers: jQuery is a popular JavaScript library that simplifies event handling and makes it more efficient. For example:

```
$("#myButton").click(function() {
  alert("Hello World!");
});
```

It's important to note that event handlers are executed in the order that they are added. So, if you have multiple handlers for a single event, they will be executed one after another.

interactive and dynamic web pages. With the right tools and a bit of practice, anyone can learn to use JavaScript for web development.

CHAPTER 6

ASYNCHRONOUS JAVASCRIPT

Callbacks, Promises, and async/await

JavaScript is a single-threaded programming language, which means that it can only process one task at a time. However, JavaScript provides several ways to perform tasks asynchronously, such as callbacks, promises, and async/await.

Callbacks are functions that are passed as arguments to other functions and are executed when a certain event occurs. For example:

```javascript
function getData(callback) {
  setTimeout(function() {
    callback("Data Received!");
  }, 1000);
}

getData(function(data) {
  console.log(data);
});
```

Promises are a more recent addition to JavaScript and provide a more elegant way to handle asynchronous tasks. A promise represents the eventual result of an asynchronous operation and can be in one of three states: fulfilled, rejected, or pending. For example:

```javascript
var promise = new Promise(function(resolve, reject) {
  setTimeout(function() {
    resolve("Data Received!");
  }, 1000);
});

promise.then(function(data) {
  console.log(data);
});
```

Async/await is a more recent feature of JavaScript and it makes working with asynchronous code more natural and similar to synchronous code. For example:

```javascript
async function getData() {
  const data = await fetch('https://api.github.com/users');
  console.log(data);
}

getData();
```

CHAPTER 7

FRAMEWORKS AND LIBRARIES

Explanation of what JavaScript is and its role in web development

JavaScript frameworks and libraries are pre-written code that can be used to help developers quickly and easily build web applications. These tools provide a set of functions and methods that can be used to perform common tasks, such as handling events, making requests to servers, and manipulating the DOM. In this chapter, you will learn about some of the most popular JavaScript frameworks and libraries and how they can be used to make your development process more efficient and effective.

React

React is a popular JavaScript library for building user interfaces. It is used to create reusable UI components and manage the state of an application. React uses a virtual DOM, which allows it to efficiently update the UI when the state of the application changes.

Vue.js

Vue.js is a popular JavaScript framework that is similar to React. It is used to create reusable UI components and manage the state of an application. Vue.js also uses a virtual DOM and provides a set of directives that can be used to bind data to the DOM.

AngularJS

AngularJS is a popular JavaScript framework for building web applications. It uses a declarative approach to building UIs and provides a set of directives that can be used to bind data to the DOM. AngularJS also provides a set of services and controllers that can be used to manage the state of an application.

jQuery

jQuery is a popular JavaScript library that provides a set of methods for manipulating the DOM, handling events, and making requests to servers. It is designed to make it easier to work with the DOM and provides a simple and consistent API that can be used across different browsers.

Bootstrap

Bootstrap is a popular CSS framework that provides a set of CSS classes that can be used to quickly and easily create responsive and stylish web pages. It provides a set of grid classes that can be used to create responsive layouts and a set of components that can be used to create forms, buttons, and other UI elements.

Using frameworks and libraries can save you a lot of time and effort when building web applications. They provide a set of tools and techniques that can be used to quickly and easily build and maintain web applications. However, it's important to remember that frameworks and libraries are not always the right solution for every project. In some cases, it's best to build your own code from scratch.

In the next chapter, you will learn about JavaScript modules and how they can be used to organize and structure your code.

Exercises:

- Research and create a simple webpage using React
- Research and create a simple webpage using Vue.js
- Research and create a simple webpage using AngularJS
- Research and create a simple webpage using Bootstrap

The above chapter gives an overview of some of the most popular javascript frameworks and libraries available, React, Vue.js, AngularJS, jQuery and Bootstrap, what they are useful for and how they can be used to improve the development process. It also includes some exercises for readers to research and practice building web pages using these tools.

CHAPTER 8
MODULES AND IMPORT/EXPORT

Explanation of what JavaScript is and its role in web development

JavaScript modules are a way to organize and reuse your code. They allow you to divide your code into smaller, more manageable pieces and to import and export specific parts of your code to other files.

ES6 introduced the import and export keywords for working with modules. The export keyword is used to make a variable, function, or class available to be imported by other files. For example:

```javascript
export function add(a, b) {
  return a + b;
}
```

The import keyword is used to import a variable, function, or class from another file. For example:

```javascript
import { add } from './math.js';
console.log(add(1, 2));
```

It's also possible to export and import the entire module using the * symbol. For example:

```js
export * from './math.js';
```

Or

```js
import * as math from './math.js';
console.log(math.add(1, 2));
```

ES modules are supported by all modern browsers and Node.js, so you don't need to use a transpiler like Babel to use them.

CHAPTER 9

JAVASCRIPT BEST PRACTICES

Explanation of what JavaScript is and its role in web development

As with any programming language, there are certain best practices that you should follow when working with JavaScript. These include:

> Using strict mode: This enables a more strict version of JavaScript, which can help to prevent common mistakes and improve security. To use strict mode, add the "use strict" statement at the beginning of your code.
>
> Declaring variables with `let` and `const`: Instead of using the `var` keyword, you should use the `let` keyword to declare variables that can be reassigned, and the `const` keyword to declare variables that cannot be reassigned.
>
> Using arrow functions: Arrow functions are a shorthand for defining functions and have a more concise syntax.

- Using template literals: Template literals are a way to create strings that include expressions, and they have a more readable syntax than traditional string concatenation.

- Using destructuring: Destructuring is a way to extract values from arrays or objects and assign them to variables.

- Using spread operator: Spread operator is a way to spread an array or object elements into a new array or object.

- Avoiding global variables: Whenever possible, you should avoid using global variables and instead use modules and closures to keep your code organized and avoid naming conflicts.

- Writing comments: Comments are an essential part of any codebase, and they help to explain what your code is doing and make it more readable to other developers.

CHAPTER 10

CONCLUSION

Explanation of what JavaScript is and its role in web development

JavaScript is a powerful and versatile programming language that is essential for building interactive and dynamic web applications. This book has provided an introduction to the basics of JavaScript, including its syntax, data types, functions, and event handling.

We've also covered more advanced topics, such as asynchronous JavaScript, JavaScript frameworks and libraries, and modules and import/export. Additionally, we've discussed best practices for writing maintainable and readable code.

As you continue to learn and work with JavaScript, you'll encounter many more features and concepts that you can use to build more complex and sophisticated applications. Remember to keep practicing and experimenting with different techniques and tools, and you'll be well on your way to becoming a proficient JavaScript developer.

ABOUT THE AUTHOR

John Facey II - I am a web developer, software engineer, and architect currently living in Dallas, Texas. I am well versed in JavaScript, Node.js, Salesforce Commerce Cloud / OCAPI, PHP, JAVA,.NET and various other languages and platforms. My interests include programming, martial arts and my dogs.

Everyone always asks me how to get started in programming so I hope this helps new developers jump into JavaScript :)

www.ingramcontent.com/pod-product-compliance
Lightning Source LLC
Chambersburg PA
CBHW040346220526
45473CB00009B/2799